SOUL CIRCLES

SOUL CIRCLES

Mandalas & Meaning

COMMENTARY BY
David H. Rosen and **Jeremy Jensen**

MANDALA ILLUSTRATIONS BY
Jeremy Jensen

FOREWORD BY
Patti Henderson

RESOURCE *Publications* · Eugene, Oregon

SOUL CIRCLES
Mandalas & Meaning

Resource Publications
An Imprint of Wipf and Stock Publishers
199 W. 8th Ave., Suite 3
Eugene, OR 97401

www.wipfandstock.com

PAPERBACK ISBN: 978-1-7252-6824-1
HARDCOVER ISBN: 978-1-7252-6825-8
EBOOK ISBN: 978-1-7252-6826-5

Manufactured in the U.S.A.   MARCH 23, 2020

Jeremy dedicates this work to his father, Kim.

David dedicates this work to his wife, Lanara.

ACKNOWLEDGEMENTS

I would like to thank David for his gentle persistence in urging me to use a creative outlet for healing, and his guidance through this part of my individuation process. I would also like to thank my wife, Chelsie, for her love and care, and her walking through this life with me.

—*Jeremy Jensen*

Jeremy Jensen's mandalas illustrate this book and are fine examples of his growth and development. Each mandala has commentaries by both authors. Jeremy is an artist and plans to become a Jungian analsyst. A heartfelt thanks to Patti Henderson for her foreword and her dedicated research into the healing aspects of mandalas. A deep bow and appreciation to James Stock, Jim Tedrick, and their staff at Wipf & Stock Publishers, who are so great to work with. I am grateful to Bonnie Sheehey and Rebekah Sinclair for their editorial assistance. Finally, I thank my wife, Lanara, for her continued support and love.

—*David Rosen*

FOREWORD

My first encounter with mandalas was when I was an undergraduate student at Texas A&M University. Dr. Rosen was teaching a meaningful class where we were tasked to look inward to discover our inner purpose towards individuation. I soon discovered that mandalas could be healing and lead to insight. When I was a graduate student studying with Dr. Rosen, I researched the healing aspects of mandalas and their use as tools to promote lasting wellbeing.

This is an important book in that it shows the value of creating mandalas as symbols of the psyche and a path for understanding our inner selves and feelings of individuation. The analysand was brave to share these with others in hopes of helping them to understand how useful they can be in healing ones' own soul. Jeremy Jensen's and Dr. Rosen's insights into the meaning are invaluable.

—*Patti Henderson*

PREFACE

This is a work of active imagination, which yields an artistic product. It is "dreaming the dream onward," according to the Jungian analyst, June Singer.[1] Mandalas are circles, often with four quadrants.[2] At times they can be squares or a circled square or a squared circle.

The analysand in this case was getting a graduate degree in counseling and expressed a desire to be a Jungian analyst. At the time, he was in his thirties, married, with two sons. He worked as a counselor in a community-based center, where he was a therapist with some difficult and disturbing cases. His wife was also in a helping profession as an occupational therapist. This individual sought treatment because, when he was younger, his father had committed suicide. He thought about his own sons, then 3 and 13, and did not want to repeat such a tragic scenario. He voiced self doubts about attaining his graduate degree because of a negative self image. Nevertheless, it was clear that he was a good father, husband, and therapist, and a very bright student. His graduate research focused on obtaining wholeness. He was embracing research as me-search. This is telling because that's what a mandala means - wholeness. Carl Jung himself wrote an insightful synopsis about mandalas.[3] Another key aspect of Carl Jung's analytic approach, active imagination, fits well with this individual because of his artistic ability and his elaborate mandalas.

The analysand did complete his degree and continues to work as a therapist.

The foreword is by Patti Henderson who did important research involving mandalas.[4]

—*David Rosen*

From the beginning of creating these mandalas, and with the process repeating with each new image, I had no idea what would come out on the page until just before the process of creation started. Sometimes a central image would come to mind, and I would place that down on the page. Other times, I would start the process with nothing in mind and the images would come afterwards. I did not know when the next mandala would come out, or if the one I was working on would be the last. During the mandala creation, I would often feel (through active imagination) that certain images, shapes or symbols wanted to be placed at certain places in the mandala or in relation to other images, shapes or symbols. The mandala creation process was inherently mysterious and rewarding. To me, much more could be written about these mandalas than is written here, and I resisted for a long time putting words to them because I think there is power in the images in and of themselves prior to interpretation.

—*Jeremy Jensen*

1. Singer, J. (1994). *Boundaries of the Soul: The Practice of Jung's Psychology.* New York: Anchor Books.

2. Bergeron, D.P., Rosen, D.H., Arnau, R.C. & Mascaro, N. (2003). Picture interpretation and Jungian typology. *The Journal of Analytical Psychology* 48: 83–99.

3. Jung, C.G. (1969). "Mandalas." In *Volume 9.1 of the Collected Works. Archetypes and the Collective Unconscious.* New York: Princeton University Press. 387–390.

4. Henderson, P, Rosen, D.H. & Mascaro, N. (2007). Empirical study on the healing nature of mandalas. *Psychology of Aesthetics, Creativity, and the Arts* 1 (3): 148–154.

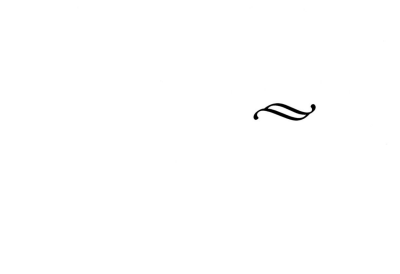

David H. Rosen

In Jeremy Jensen's first mandala, there is a square with a circle inside, and the Star of David embraces the central red circle. In addition to the Star of David, there are 8 red circles around the square. There are also several other circles in this drawing. So there are multiple mandalas, since mandala means circle. It's noteworthy that there is a sun circle in the top right corner, which is the future quadrant. Note also that this drawing is quite faint in color and form.

The analysand grew up in a community of Mormons, but because of his mother, he was not raised in the faith. I didn't realize there was a connection between Judaism and Mormonism until I attended a Jungian meeting in Salt Lake City and a Mormon Jungian analyst invited us to visit their Temple and have lunch in Brigham Young's home. When I noticed a large Star of David at the top of the Temple, I was told that Mormons believe they are one of the lost tribes of Israel. Thus it becomes clear why the Star of David appears in this analysand's first image, as well as several future images.

Jeremy Jensen

I had been seeing David for just over a year, and in that time I had avoided his promptings to create art as part of the therapeutic process. A major factor in this avoidance was self-doubt, that voice of self-doubt would say, "you can't create something meaningful. Whatever you do, it will be crap." I needed to remind myself that things grow from crap, or it could be also known as the "prima materia." Once I set self-judgement aside, the images started to come forth.

The most salient features of this mandala to me are the green Star of David in the center, and the eight points around it making a 16 petaled Rose. I did not think of this until I began writing, but the Star of David and the Rose, are similar enough to David Rosen's name. Maybe an unconscious symbolic pun? Maybe some sort of feeling of identification with David, the analyst and healer? I am not sure. However, at the face of it, I personally think the Star of David seems to be balanced and positive; it feels like a beneficent starting point. The triangle pointing upwards to the sky and spirit, and the triangle pointing downwards to the Earth and soul.

Rosen

It's readily apparent in his second mandala that this individual is already centering himself. The difference between this and his first image is striking, as this one already has far bolder and darker colors, and braver, more defined shapes than the first. To begin here, green is the color of growth, and it is thus noteworthy that he begins his journey open to development, like a strong, green tree. He identifies with the tree, which Jung describes in his writings as a symbol of the Self. The numerology of six appears in this drawing with the dots along the edge of the circle. First, this relates to early trauma, perhaps around the age of six, and it's also likely that family figures are represented by the dots. Age six is also an important year because if the individual feels inherently good about him or herself at that time, they can more easily actualize their potential. This matches with the analysand's history, as he was was identified as gifted in the educational system. In addition, a circle represents not only wholeness but also the feminine. This is interesting since, in numerology, even numbers, and particularly the number six, represent feminine energies like caring, loving, and healing. This is why six is also called the "motherhood number."[1] So here we have a big circle which is feminine, and six small circles that are feminine. Below the tree lies an infinity sign, which signifies wholeness and finding oneself. Interestingly, there are two triangles outside the central circle. Triangles are considered masculine because they have three sides, and odd numbers are masculine. The triangles are also located outside the feminine circle, as those two energies have not been integrated.

Jensen

As I was suffering from bouts of insomnia, David advised that when I couldn't sleep, I should try making a mandala. So, this mandala occurred at 4:00 in the morning after I had been up for some time with acute anxiety. I was unprepared with materials, and I made this with a used scrap of paper from my graduate program. The only drawing implement I could find was my 5-year-old son's green Crayola marker. As I sat in front of the paper, an evergreen tree came clearly to my mind's eye. My immediate association with the tree were the many pine trees in Oregon. I also thought of "ever green" as meaning continually alive, immortal. Though, I also associate green with jealousy, money, or inexperience. Green may mean health in plants, thought a green complexion in a person may mean sickliness. Overall at the time, the evergreen tree felt strong, sturdy and positive.

After I had put the tree down on the page, it felt as though the image drew itself. I felt right to have the tree encircled by six points (which could be connected into another Star of David), and below an infinity symbol (which is the first instance of a repeating theme through the series of mandalas). I was struck by at the time was mysterious scribbled columns to either side of the circle, which appeared to me to have eyes at the base of each. Two columns or trees also become a repeating pattern through this series of mandalas. It also felt appropriate to place two upwards pointing triangles at the 4 and 6 o'clock points on the circle (active principles, connecting to spirit). After I finished the mandala, I felt a sense of relief from my anxiety and was able to go to sleep.

1. Decoz, H. & Monte, T. (1994). *Numerology: Key to your Inner Self*. New York: Perigee.

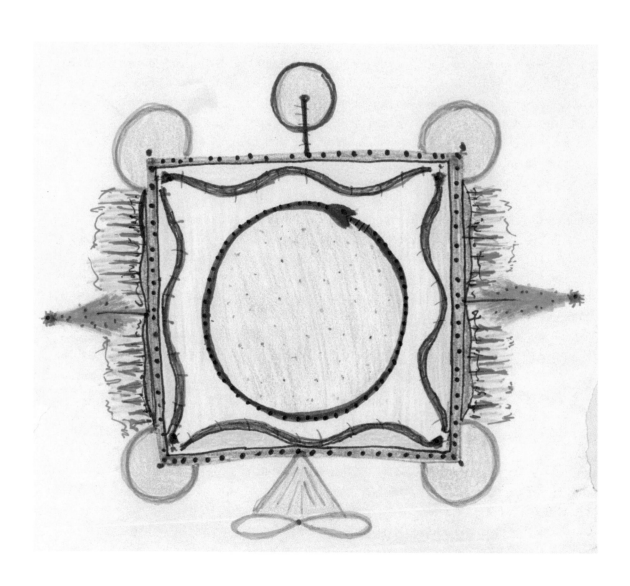

Rosen

You can see how this third mandala is more balanced, which reflects the patient's immediate therapeutic progress. This mandala represents wholeness and his overcoming emotional difficulties. In the center is an ouroboros, which is an ancient symbol of a snake eating its own tail. It signifies infinity and wholeness (which is again highlighted in the bottom of the mandala), as well as death and rebirth. The five orange circles, mirrored by the five serpents, relates to trauma around age five, which clearly is being faced. The orange trees in the green forest perhaps indicate balancing both family and education.

At this time, he had a dream of three animals—a big buck, a bobcat, and a wolf. All three were white in color with gold highlights and were larger than they would be in real life. The bobcat attacked his right side, just above the liver, which is significant because of a later dream in which he has a liver transplant. He was able to take them on with a knife and prevent his own death. Concurrently, he was doing well in his studies, but doubted that he would be able to graduate. However, it seemed to me that he was right on track to finish his degree, which I emphasized. The blue square symbolizes his masculine identity and feeling more secure as a father and husband, and that he could achieve his dream.

Jensen

The first image that came forth in this mandala was the Ouroboros, the snake eating its own tail, as it encapsulates the center of the image, which is dotted with a purple background. This seemed to me like a starry sky, or the cosmos. To me, the Ouroboros is a symbol for the living universe— life feeds off itself to continue manifestation in its multitudinous forms. The Ouroboros appears to be moving clockwise, while there are four other serpents are moving counterclockwise. The four serpents inside the box seem like they are holding dynamic energy of change, otherwise the mandala seems static or stable. I also think of these serpents as representing growth and change, as the serpent sheds its skin. There is a need to be on guard around the serpents, as they may be venomous.

A blue square: straight, linear, and rational has reappeared (see mandala #1). Also, the evergreen tree has been transformed into two orange Christmas trees on either side of the square. I think of childhood excitement on Christmas day, waking to see which gifts were underneath the Christmas tree. More gruesomely, in relation to this, I think of the myth of Attis where he castrated himself underneath a pine tree because he was turned insane by a jealous Cybele. Attis, like Christ, is a vegetative god who dies to be reborn anew. There are growing green forests all around the Christmas trees. It seems there is an indication towards the threat of pain and insanity and ultimately death. Though, there is the hope of gifts to come, and new life to flourish. As I fear moving forward, I was reminded of the verse from the gospel of Thomas, "If you bring forth what is within you, what you bring forth will save you. If you do not bring forth what is within you, what you do not bring forth will destroy you."

Rosen

In this fourth drawing, the healing serpents appear again, surrounded by green growth, and the mountains of graduate school and self-affirmation, which he must climb. The two colorful trees with the Stars of David also signify balance. In addition to Judaism and Mormonism, the six-pointed Star of David is central in Hinduism. It's a universal symbol that integrates the masculine sky with the feminine earth. The reoccurring theme of the infinity is at the bottom of the image. The oval at the top with the three dots may represent his sense of well-being and wholeness at age three before the trauma. The maze is what he is presently going through and what he hopes to find his way out of.

Jensen

The central image of the purple mountain came to my mind's eye to begin with. This mountain held the same coloring as the cosmos previously in the center of mandala #3. I see this as the holy mountain. Like the upwards pointing triangle, the mountain peak is pointing towards the sky and the lofty. The peak is where spirit meets matter. I think it's interesting that the cosmos is contained in the mountain. The mountain is to me, both a destination for a journey, as well as the center of the internal psyche. There are also seven peaks in the mountain range, a significant number to me, a lucky number. Below there are two serpents facing one another, whose bodies comprise a labyrinth. A part of the labyrinth leads into the bottom of the mountain. I must find my way through the maze to reach the holy mountain. Above the mountain, two snakes facing away from one another. Their bodies are vines holding fruit (possibly grapes). The growth of fruit is similar to the gifts underneath the Christmas tree, they are naturally grown gifts. At the base of the trees, two triangles have returned, as in Mandala #2, though this time downward facing, the receptive principle pointing to the ground. Also, the blue square outlines this mandala, though it seemed important to leave a section between two point opened. Maybe there is a break in rigid boundaries opening to deeper consciousness? I felt very positive about this image when I made it, it seemed as though the process was coming easier. Although, I couldn't quite verbalize what it was, it felt as though there was some sort of movement or change happening within myself.

Rosen

In this fifth mandala, he feels more confident as a man, husband, and father. Again, the symbol of the infinity occurs.[2] It's noteworthy that the symbol of the female is featured inside the yellow circles on the upper left and lower right corners. Yellow symbolizes courage and hope. He softened the red of rage and anger with yellow and orange. The Star of David again appears in the image. The spiral in the bottom left side of the mandala represents him coming out of depression and facing his rage. The figure in the middle is a compass made up of ouroboros and serpents. Again, the psyche is integrating and healing itself.

Jensen

This mandala felt creatively much more chaotic when compared to the previous mandalas. It felt appropriate to place many symbols, thought I won't describe all of them. I might say the most significant is the presence for the first time in the series, was the symbol of Mercury in the bottom right corner. Mercury/Hermes is the messenger god traveling between the human world and the divine, or the psychopomp that guides souls to the afterlife. He is a god of communication, and the of the roads where ideas more easily traveled from one area to another. He is also a trickster. I have a personal affiliation with the ideas associated with Hermes/Mercury and feel like he is a good aspect of the self to act as guide through the mandala creation process. The Mercury glyph will continually return throughout the series. I would like to also point out the eye in the bottom left corner. I associate the eye with consciousness, and it is through the eye all these images are communicated in a nonverbal language. The blue square returns, and appears to be transforming further, becoming more unstable and with more breaks in continuity (this time at the corners). Again, the Ouroboros appears, though this time smaller, and moving counterclockwise. Afterwards, I thought the silver circle around the Ouroboros reminded me of a tower (or possibly a mountain) looking from the top down, and it had a door opening at the bottom of the circle. This mandala felt as though I was allowing myself to get more comfortable with chaos; there was little of the self-judgment I had in the beginning of the series regarding their creation .

2. Ronnberg, A. & Martin, K. (2010). *The Book of Symbols.* Cologne: Taschen Press.

24

Rosen

In the sixth mandala, the tree of life symbolizes stability and self-actualization. At this time, he had a dream that he was on a green hill and had turned into a maiden, which is his anima or feminine side. In the image above, the worker bees on either side of the tree and all the honey comb underscore his being productive at home and in his education. The flowers on either side, which are pollinated by the bees, represent fertility and growth. The serpents going in different directions symbolize balance, healing, and sensitivity.

Jensen

A tree centers this image as in mandala number two, though it is no longer an evergreen tree. This tree comes had been a recurring image in active imaginations, and dreams I had. I would imagine feelings of safety and peace as I relaxed leaning against this tree as it sat upon a green hill. The tree was a large and solid counterpart of myself. Something that grew out of a tiny seed but was much larger and long-lived than my human self. The tree is also a symbol of myself, it is the Axis Mundi, the axis on which the world rotates (the same center-point symbolism could be said of the holy mountain from mandala #4). The bees were a new and positive presence, they are busy collecting nectar and making honey, and they pollenate the flowers. Honey is sweet and gold, it is antiseptic and can preserve many things. The production of honey is in preparation to make it through the winter months. I could see honey as liquid sunlight; sunlight filtered through flowers and by the work of bees. There is a living and happy feeling to me with this mandala, but something substantial and strong, as if foundation has been laid. The blue square has transformed into a square particles or flowers, more permeable and more impermanent. With that there is also at the top of the image a figure, angelic with golden wings watching in protection from above.

Rosen

At the top of the door depicted in this seventh mandala is the Latin expression, "Vocatus atque non vocatus Deus aderit," which means "Called or not called, God is present." This saying is at the top of my front door, which he would see every time he visited at my home office. He puts this threshold (thresh and hold) in his drawing in the paternal and maternal quadrants, respectively. There are also two triangles with opposite serpents. It's noteworthy that serpents are symbols of all healing professions. As Jung says, holding the tension of the opposites is the key to health. This can be seen by the skull depicting death and the lightbulb signifying life and rebirth. Also noteworthy is the ankh in the center, which symbolizes life and truth. The rainbow is significant as it indicates reward both in family and profession in the future.

Jensen

This mandala came first to me as a word: "threshold," then as the image of the door. This image feels like it is the entry point for the deeper exploration; the gateway for initiation. Threshold was split into two words: "thresh" and "hold." Threshing is the act of beating a crop to separate the seed from the stalk, and here in the mandala underneath the word, thresh, there is a sheaf of wheat. The way forward comes with some thrashing, some pain. An angelic hand is holding a key which is also in the form of the Mercury glyph; the hand could also be holding a lightbulb, a light of conscious awareness. The door is purple and dotted, similar to the cosmos in previous images. Above the door, written in blood, was a term in Latin that was above both David's doorway, as well as C.G. Jung's: "Vocatus atque non vocatus deus aderit" (called or uncalled, God is present). This saying was on the one hand honoring the place of the guides on this journey, as well as a ward against my own self-doubt in life. Regardless of my doubts about myself the process of transformation and relationship between the ego and Self was becoming more apparent and deepening. It is a call to trust myself and trust the process. I imagine myself as the door and the thing that walks through the door. I also see the overall imagery of this mandala as an invitation to let die the aspects that of the self that need to die, and open the door into new life.

Rosen

At the bottom of this eighth, drawing, it states, "In all Chaos there is a Cosmos, in all Disorder a secret Order." The analysand is noting what is central in chaos theory and also what happens in Jungian analytic therapy. It's clear that he is integrating masculine and feminine inside a mandorla (enclosing the human being where the two circles meet), and has drawn a double mandala. The ages of eleven and twenty-two, represented in the numbers, are significant. As Jung observed, one's identity crystallizes around eleven and one becomes an adult around twenty-two.

Again, the double triangles (which can be integrated to make a Star of David) appear on the top of the colorful triangles and the downward pointing triangle represents the struggle of integrating his anima. He dreamt around this time that he was under water and drowning. What this represents is his ego dying, or egocide and transformation. He commented that the reason he came to see me was so that he would not commit suicide but egocide.[3]

Jensen

In this mandala, there is a man (an image of myself) who is on the threshold of a mandorla. This character seems impersonal without personality or character. It was cut from a body diagram from an autopsy report. With that, there are several wounds that represent either psychological or physical (and both) traumas I have experienced throughout my life. I feel like I am here beginning to confront and accept these wounds as significant aspects of myself and history. I also see an obvious dichotomy between the John Doe depersonalization of the autopsy image, and the inflation of the Christ imagery (with the wounds, mandorla). Though both in this case may represent false self.

The mandorla is made of two circles, and show the repeating pattern of the blue, red, white and yellow dots on purple, which has been a symbol for the cosmos. This time the dots are bigger, and the two circles remind me of cells dividing. Possibly an embryo is forming.

The orange Christmas trees appear again with gold and silver stars at their tops, and two columns with a B and J. At the time, I am not sure why I put these down on the page. I was vaguely familiar with them through the tarot (in the Priestess card), and ritual ceremony rites (such as in Freemasonry), but I did not have knowledge on their symbolic meaning. I think the duality of the pair is the most important aspect. There is a tension of opposites held between the two columns. Maybe these are a progression of the scribbled columns in mandala #2, and the pine trees in #3, #4, and in this mandala.

Eleven and Twenty-Two are symbols of personal myth for me. When I was 25 years old, I had a significant dream. The culminating point of the dream was when I asked an ancient and powerfully wise being when I would die. It told me 11/22. In the intervening years the numbers have become to have rich symbolism to me, overall pointing to the process of death and rebirth, decay and growth/renewal. This has of course been a recurring theme in these mandalas.

3. Rosen, D.H. (2002). *Transforming Depression.* York Beach, ME: Nicolas-Hays.

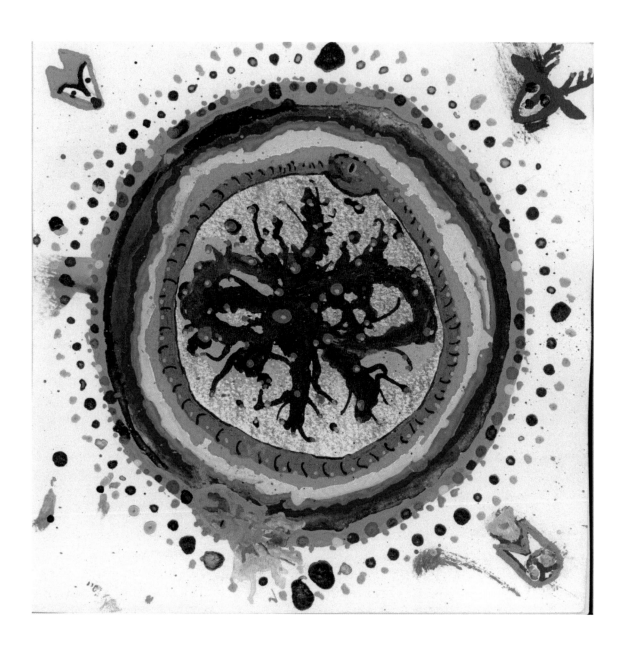

Rosen

At this time, during the painting of this ninth mandala, he had a fear of failing and being seen. I countered this with the idea that maybe he was afraid of success and actually wanted to be seen and accepted by others. Despite all of these conflicts, he was realizing that he had to speak with his own voice and accept himself. A circular ouroboros appears again in this mandala, along with three helping animals: the sly fox, the strong stag, and the wise owl.

He is accepting the rage he experienced with his own father, which is depicted in the middle of the image. As I pointed out to him, this shadow energy contains all the elements of creativity and self-realization. To test himself at this time, he went on a Vipassana meditation retreat for ten days, which required him to be completely silent. I thought this was significant as it allowed him to silently accept himself without feedback from others. Additionally, while on the retreat, the analysand had a mystical experience relating to his family lineage, which is interesting because he found out after the retreat that his wife was pregnant with his second son. Much later he wrote the following, very lovely haiku.

> gaze drawn to the west
> deer opposed the rising sun
> we are all running

I thought he was identifying with me and something that I love.[4]

Jensen

The image that first came to me for this mandala, was a black swirling shape. It was my pain and shadow. Parts of myself that I was ashamed of, disgusted by, and wanted to reject. The black mass came together around another infinity symbol. Then I saw that this part needed to be encapsulated, and this came out first in the red serpent Ouroboros, then the colors of the rainbow. And finally, it is encircled by a golden dragon Ouroboros with the colors of the rainbow on its spine. This is the first mandala that felt truly dark and dangerous to me as I was making it. It brought up unresolved grief from childhood, and from my father's unexpected death. I associate the dragon as a protective and integrative power, though it is dangerous itself. When I had finished the circles, I still felt like the mandala was not contained. I then placed the three animals around the periphery as protectors, the fox, stag, and owl. It also felt important to leave the bottom left corner blank. Though I felt anxiety and discomfort as I made this mandala, afterwards I felt a sense of relief.

4. Rosen, D.H. & Weishaus, J. (2014). *The Healing Spirit of Haiku*. Eugene, OR: Resource Publications.

Rosen

Just before painting this tenth, colorful mandala, the analysand had a significant dream of having a liver transplant. The liver functions to clean out all of the toxins in one's body. He had had a drinking problem, which is considered chronic partial suicide. However, he gave this up when he was doing the analytic work. Respecting the liver is a way of respecting life, since the root of the word comes from the german verb, leber, "to live." He would also talk and read about shamanism, an ancient practice of death and rebirth. The downward triangle means that he is working on integrating his feminine side. The eye in the middle of the triangle represents his new identity. The black symbolizes the ground of all the traumatic energy, which he now is utilizing to help himself. The upward triangle in the Hindu hexagram symbolizes father sky, and the downward, mother earth. So here again we have an integrated, balanced symbol. And, when taken together, the two triangles create a Star of David.

Jensen

Underlying the beginning of this image was an explosion of black. The black mass of the previous image had gone beyond its original encapsulation. In the center, is the solar eye of consciousness being brought to bear on the pain that came forth and expanded from the previous image. The eye perpendicular to the horizontal line can make a cross, as well. The seven colors of the rainbow along with gold are forming the downwards facing triangle. The seven colors are the colors of apparent outward existence, the field of vision. With this mandala, I was becoming more aware of personal meaning given to colors. Behind the main triangle there are black, white, and red form a counterbalancing triangle pointing upwards. I felt like there was a progression in white, black, and red. White symbolize purity; on these pages it is the underlying screen that everything else is built from. Possibly equivalent to the field of consciousness. Black came next, and it is the darkening, the shadow to the light. It also begins to give form where there was none before. White and black form the initial duality. Red seemed to come next in the progression, and to me it represented life (as with the color of blood). This brings a dynamism to black and white, both anger and love I associate with red.

This mandala was visually less contained in its blackness than the previous mandala, it felt like something may be in movement and might be under transformation. I also felt some particular mysteriousness about the image.

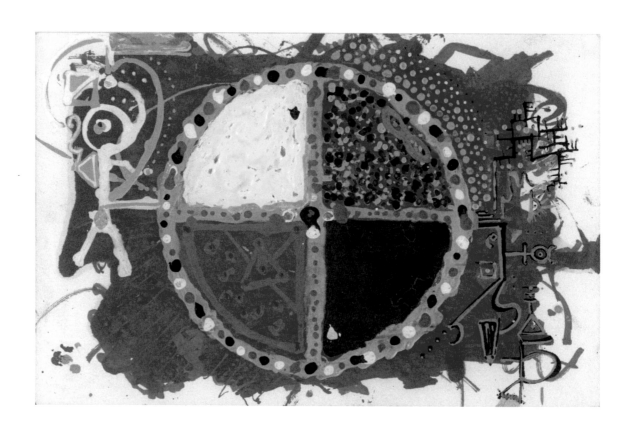

Rosen

In this eleventh drawing, a classic mandala, he is integrating past trauma, represented here by black and red, which acts as the ground of this image. The white depicted in the upper left hand corner represents his new inner father figure and the possibility of accepting himself in his graduate education. The upper left quadrant is the father quadrant, and the lower right corner represents the mother quadrant.[5] The black and white are balanced on either side of the circle as a yin yang. The smaller circles on the outer edge of the larger circle symbolize wholeness. The bottom left quadrant represents the unconscious, and in this case, repressed rage, and the future is in the opposite position, in the upper right hand corner. It is filled with bright possibilities. Note that the black, white, and red dots within the main circle each number twenty one, which, recall, is a critical age.

Jensen

The white, black, red progression continued in this mandala. The blackness prominent in the last image has transformed to a background of red in this image. I could say as further associations with black are fear, darkness, and coldness. The abyss. Wounding and trauma. Red is life and matters of the heart, for better or worse (as state previously: anger and love). Red is fiery. To me this mandala could be saying that I am bringing to life wounding that I had kept in the dark.

White, black and red are prominent in the central mandala, a golden circle, or wheel, or egg. Blue and purple particles with another infinity symbol comprise the fourth quadrant. This could be something in phase of formation, or it could be the ultimate dissolution of the blue squares from the earlier mandalas (there are no more blue squares in the remaining images). Also, on the perimeter there is black/gold and white/silver in balance, reminiscent of the colors of the Boaz and Jachin columns of Mandala #8. The symbols and lines on these were esoteric and alien, which made me think that there was something outside my ego-consciousness at work in catalyzing transformation.

---

5. Op. cite n.2.

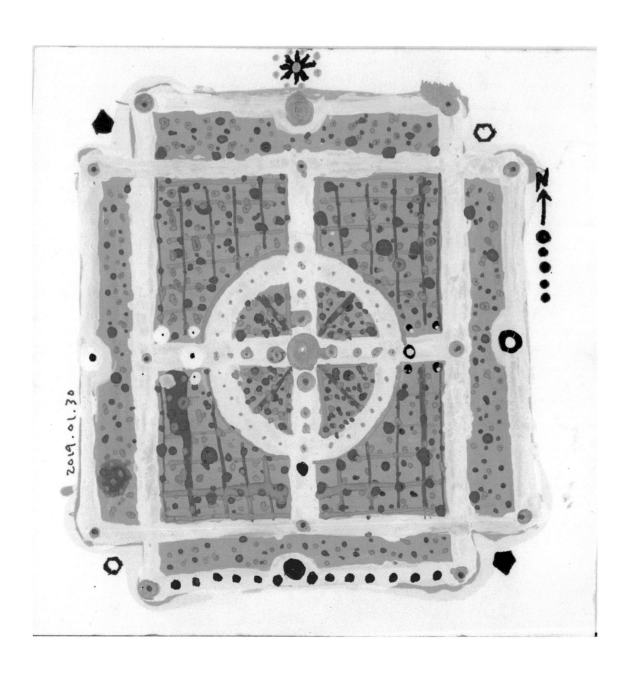

Rosen

This twelfth mandala was taken directly from a dream which follows:

In the dream, the analysand was in a city park with people playing a pick-up game of soccer. There were four different teams playing one another simultaneously. He felt as though he was on his own team, with nobody passing him the ball and he not passing it to anyone else. It was really difficult to get the ball, and when he did, he could only kick it once or twice before it was taken the other way. The ball was kicked all over the place but nobody made any goals.

In the image above, the red circles represent fellow players, while the north end represents the goal.

Even though, from within the dream, the image represents frustrated or uncompleted goals, from an analysts perspective, this image is one of growth, development, and centering. It again represents a compass, balance, and finding direction. The analysand still doubted his ability to graduate and finish his thesis, which was already about forty percent complete by this point. Unlike the previous mandala with the green maze, this is a symbol of completion. No longer a labyrinth, he is finding his way. This is clearly a hopeful drawing. The bottom row of smaller red dots, numbering thirteen, signifies the difficulty and promise of adolescence. The two larger red dots represent the coalescing of his identity.

Jensen

This image was unusual in the series as it came directly from a dream (normally they came first through active imagination): "I'm in a city and people are playing a game of soccer. It's four different sides all against each another. I am playing alone, the only player on my team, so I don't pass it to anyone nor is it passed to me. It's extremely difficult to get control over the ball, and when I do, I can only kick it once or twice before it's taken the other way. It's kicked all different directions, and no one seems to make a goal. The north side is my goal."

I saw this dream as a mandala from above, and the mandala here was the representation of that. I felt like the green playing field was a repetition of a pattern that had manifested in other dreams, usually as a green hill (mentioned in mandala #12 description). The green also recalls the evergreen from mandala #2, and the green labyrinth and vines of mandala #4. My intended goal is the north, and on the mandala, it is moving from red in the south, or black and white to the east and west, towards the gold in the north. I associate the north with both the north pole, and the north star, Polaris. Again, central points around which the world or the cosmos appears to rotate, permanence.

Rosen

This thirteenth mandala inside a mandala encompasses a scary figure, inspired by the goddess Chhinnamasta, who cuts her own head off so that so that her life-blood can feed two consorts. She is a goddess represents contradictions, for example, life giver and life taker. Additionally, as he was imagining this goddess, the god Odin also came to mind, as indicated by the two ravens and the death under the world tree. The male and female gods become one in the androgynous figure who is depicted here. The serpents coming out of the head of Chhinnamasta are being eaten by the crows, who have both peace, depicted by white, and rage, depicted by red, in their wings. Out of all of this chaos and destruction, he is integrating and standing firm on the feminine earth. The Star of David and the Eye of Horus, a symbol of protection, power, and good health, figure on the top of the mandala. He is facing the destructive forces with protection and stability. In this drawing, the genitals are covered by red (anger), which often is tied to abuse.

Jensen

I feel like the mandalas turned a corner in depth, meaning, and personal impact beginning with this image. The previous images had mostly been on smaller paper (5.5"x8.5"), and this image and all following were on much larger paper (11"x14"). The image that came to me in the beginning was again of the character from mandala #8 underneath the tree from mandala #6. The image in my mind was of the character decapitating himself, following the imagery of a Hindu goddess named Chhinnamasta, who like Hermes, I have had a strange affinity with for several years. In Chhinnamasta imagery, she is seen holding her own severed head, while life-blood issues forth to feed her and her two consorts. She is also dancing on a lotus, and a copulating couple (Shiva/Shakti), which is usually on a green hill. As I saw the character decapitated in my mind, two ravens appeared in place of the two consorts. This made me think of the Norse god, Odin, who I had a little familiarity with. Odin has two ravens named 'thought' and 'memory.' Odin has one eye, like the character in the image (one eye to see externally, and one eye to see the internal or the invisible). Odin hanged himself underneath the world tree and is known as the god of the gallows. Odin sacrificed himself to himself. I was unaware until after this that there is a connection between Hermes and Odin, and they were equated when the Romans encountered the people of northern Europe. Wednesday is named for both Odin and Hermes.

I was struck by this, and then my personal conflation of Hermes/Odin with Chhinnamasta, and the tree and green hill that had arisen many times in my thought before. To me, this image speaks to the need for self-sacrifice, and the importance of removing the intellect from its throne, to live more fully from the heart, and to let the heart sustain. This image could appear to be gruesome, however, it feels hopeful to me—like something being born anew on a spring day. I felt rejuvenated after making this image. I was also surprised, it felt like it was better artwork than I expected myself to be capable of.

Rosen

This fourteenth image represents the coming together of life, death, and rebirth. There are two mandalas (one inside the other), as well as a mandorla (two overlapping mandalas). Again, the tree of life appears in the middle of the middle with the giver and taker of life on either side, depicted in black and white. The baby signifies new identity, which comes out of the fertilization of the egg and the snake-like sperm represented in the drawing. This shows the recurring theme of integrating the masculine and the feminine. The black hands of death in the bottom of the mandala hold new life in the baby. The two figures, yin and yang, hold the tension of the opposites.

Jensen

I see this image as the direct counterpoint to the previous image, feeling like the underworld version. The main colors are black, white, and red (as well as grey). The tree returns but is now barren. The two cloaked figures seem threatening to me. They seem as if they are watching over a sacrifice of the baby in the middle. The sacrifice in the previous image was given freely and taken by the self. The baby cannot choose to sacrifice itself. Though, the baby could also be viewed as being held aloft in a new birth. The center could be a sperm and egg, or a wanderer (both Hermes and Odin were wanderers) walking into a red sun. Out of destruction, something is being conceived.

The black cloaked figure came clearly to me as a figure I have seen before. It represented fear and death, similar to the grim reaper (or similarly, the dementors from the Harry Potter series). I won't describe the experience here, but this character had manifested itself to me when I was twelve years old. This was after a particularly difficult time in my life, and a feeling of abandonment from my father. The image of the sacrifice of the baby could be related to feelings of abandonment by my father as well, my parents divorced when I was eighteen months old. This image carried the feelings of that grim reaper character, feeling awful and fearful to me. Though, there was the possibility of hope within those negative feelings.

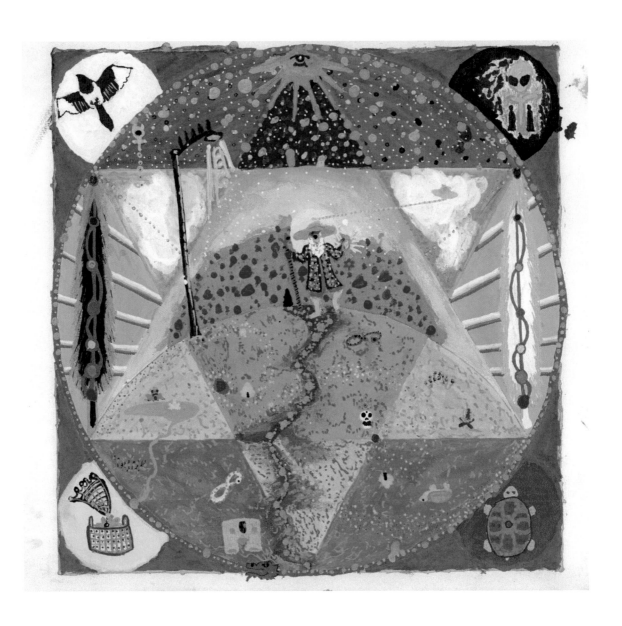

Rosen

In the top corner of this fifteenth mandala, black and white circles contain a magpie and an alien, and in the bottom circles we find a fishing net and a turtle. These indicate spirit, confronting evil, fishing to find his true self, and the slow moving, creative, healing symbol of the turtle. The mandala focuses on containing many opposites—healing ponds, infinity, an upside down turtle, fire representing purification, an ouroboros, serpents in trees on either side, clouds, and constellations. There is the integration of the father sky with earth mother. In the center is a foreign, new Self, heading down a pathway toward a castle entrance, in search of acceptance. There is a light coming out of streetlamp on the left hand side, even as the street light also looks like the grim reapers scythe, representing both death and new life.

Jensen

This image brings joy to my heart. There is a wise old man or wizard, walking energetically over the green hill as the sun rises. He is holding the serpent as a staff and holding a lantern with a Star of David hanging from it. It is possibly the figure from mandala #13 reborn triumphant. The character also reminded me of Tom Bombadil from J.R.R. Tolkien's Lord of the Rings. There are multiple sources of enlightenment present: the halo, the lantern, and the pink beam originating from the UFO, the sun, and a streetlight (which also could be a reaper's scythe). There are five cloaked figures perched on the streetlight, and another in front of the sun (though that also looks like a doorway to me). There is gold along the path the figure is walking down, and the all-seeing eye (the Eye of Providence) is raining gold and silver down from the night's sky. The pine trees have returned, the same colors as the columns, and look to be speaking to the oscillating change from one to the other like the Kundalini energy flowing through the chakras. After finishing this image, I felt as though I could call on the positive energy of the playful old wise man if I felt like I was in the underworld again.

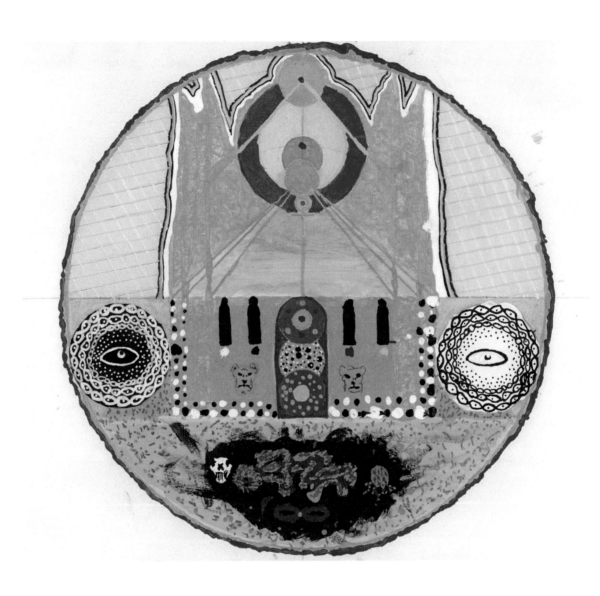

Rosen

Now, in the sixteenth drawing, he is in the castle (which looks strikingly like a church), which also contains a pyramid, a symbol of stability. The feminine symbol is at the top of the pyramid. He has integrated both eyes of the feminine and the masculine. There are other integrated aspects of the drawing as well. The red of anger is tempered with yellow, courage, to form orange. Below the sadness of death and destruction contains a green forest with pathways and a red infinity symbol. The lions in front of the castle also represent courage.

Jensen

The previous image had a castle along the path, and this image came to look both like a castle or a cathedral to me. The four black figures were both windows (or called loopholes in castles), and cloaked figures similar to the large figures in mandala #14, and the smaller figures in mandala #15. The four figures here stand above the progression of white, black, red, and now yellow. I had come to realize that these were colors of the four states of alchemy or could be the four bodily humors. The four corners, or four directions. The lions are guardians of the threshold into the chapel, the door has three circles on it, the upper one containing dots that could be made into another Star of David. Within the chapel, there looks to be a pyramid (upwards pointing triangle), and another alignment of circles.

Possibly into an astrological alignment, but also it looks to be somewhat egg-like to me. In the foreground, underneath the green hill, there is a green man buried in the fetal position. There is a bear skull at his head and a perennial bulb at his feet; the promise of rebirth. This image was another that felt to be on the dangerous side, and the title "The Chapel Perilous" came to mind. The Chapel Perilous is referred to in the Grail Legend, but I will make my own association with the term. It holds a powerful mystery, that can be entrancing. The danger is losing oneself trying to understand the mystery, driving oneself mad. An antidote to something so serious, could be humor.

Rosen

This seventeenth image is of the Buddha. This symbol indicates self-realization and balance as well as life, since Buddha became his true self rather than escaping through suicide. In his left hand (recall the left is the feminine side), the Buddha holds a crystal ball which symbolizes guidance and empowerment. However, at the same time, his left eye is covered. Was he blind to a feminine vision up until this time, or has he developed a more profound and empowered vision through analysis. His third eye or spiritual eye is illuminated while being blind in his left eye. The Buddha's heart (which is notably in the center, rather than its anatomical location) is a Star of David with green, orange, and pink. He is sitting on a rainbow colored lotus with a crown floating above his head. The crow symbols have returned, but now they each have a healing serpent in their mouth.

Jensen

Here is another joyous image to me. This was mostly taken from visionary experience I had had about a year prior to making this image. This experience came on quite suddenly and rapturously. I had the feeling of being let in on the cosmic joke, which I had not been privy to before. I also had the feeling that the universe was conspiring in my favor (pronoia as opposed to paranoia). I also sensed that below appearances, the universe was pure being, bliss, and consciousness. I felt like I was the character depicted in this image, the Laughing Buddha, or Hotei. The experience was brief, but it left an indelible positive mark on my psyche.

This image also progresses and integrates some personal mythological motifs. The figure has an eye patch, like Odin, and his two ravens return. I imagined the figure's rope belt to be the red Ouroboros from previous mandalas. His pants have similar markings and coloring as the green hill or playing field. He is wearing robes with similar to the purple cosmos motif in the mountains and the door. This is the first appearance of the diamond, which to me represents pure, solidified, and clear consciousness, a symbol for the higher self. Also, this figure has more personality, less "John Doe" than the figure in mandalas #8 and #13.

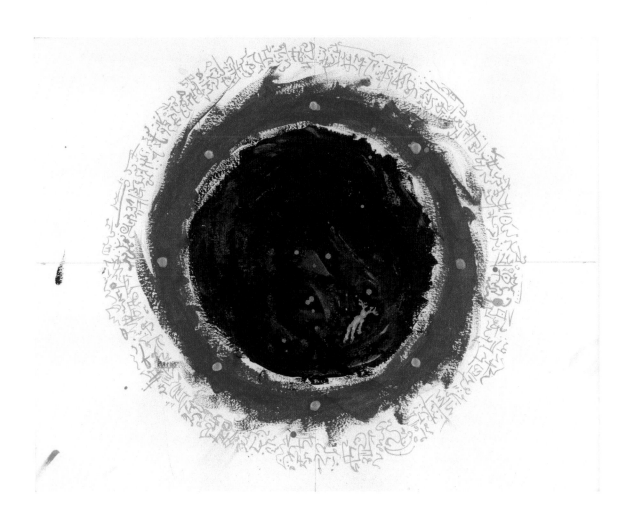

48

Rosen

This eighteenth image contains three mandalas. The central mandala is black, or feminine, yin, with a wandering entity, a therianthropic stag-human which intregrates human and non-human and which is also in the feminine, maternal quadrant. There it is being nutured and reborn. It is heading toward the future quadrant (the upper right). Perhaps we could say that the white represents another mandala, a threshold mandala, between the black and the red. The red mandala signifies passion and anger. In the red mandala there are eight yellow dots, pointing toward something happening around age eight. Surrounding both of these mandalas is a golden mandala in another language, with possible Asian and Egyptian symbols.

Jensen

Like a pendulum these mandalas have been swinging back and forth between beneficent and maleficent. This one is another negative, threatening feeling image to me. The figure in the central mandala is small and appears to be being engulfed by the dark abyss. The red, black and white circles could make a consuming mouth. This image seems to be representing trauma and wounding. The small figure in the black abyss could be therianthropic, it looks like it could be a man with antlers, or maybe it is a deer. The deer or antlers are more symbols of rebirth and regeneration, as deer shed their antlers every winter to regrow them each spring. Maybe the figure is being dissolved, maybe it is a fetus in development. The angelic or alien script around the outside seems to me to be another form of unseen guidance and protection.

Rosen

This nineteenth mandala integrates many of the past symbols. For example, in the top left and right are sun and moon. There are orange trees or candles with flames atop. On either side of these are four snow-capped mountains (and four is a feminine number). The helping animals, fox and stag, also reappear. The opposing figures in the central rainbow mandala are also familiar. Even though they represent opposing forces, they also connect to the integreted symbol of the Star of David with the earth in the center. The dark figure symbolizes the feminine and she holds a scepter, and the light figure on the right holds a caduceus. Underneath are a holy grail and a beehive, which are both symbols of integration. The hive, of course, is the place where all the worker bees get their theses finished. In the smaller mandala at the top there is a coptic cross with a golden baby attached through an ambilical cord, symbolizing rebirth and his new spiritual self. The checkerboard sections indicate further integration.

Jensen

The possible pregnancy theme from the last image shows up in multiple forms in this image. Top and center, there is an embryo connected to the center of the cross by umbilical cord at the top of the image. The embryo could be growing in the face of the suffering of the cross; it could be manifesting in real world and the four directions and four dimensions. At the bottom of the image there is a green woman giving birth to flowers. She is in the same area as the green man buried in the fetal position in mandala #16. And whereas the black and white cloaked figures in mandala #14 had appeared to be threatening, in this image they reappear, and they feel positive and hopeful to me. They seem to be in some sort of ceremony, possibly a marriage ceremony. They are connecting their hands within the Star of David and drop of blue and red blood are being caught in the grail beneath them, which is atop a beehive that has seven tiers (the doorway of the beehive also could be another black cloaked figure). The sun is on the side of the black cloaked figure, and the moon on the side of the white cloaked figure. The change in feeling towards these figures, to me is an indication of growth. From one perspective, the figure was a threat and dangerous, from another perspective it was showing me something that I could learn from, and it was an ally. As I was making this image, I felt as though I was becoming more grounded in myself, and generally positive about myself.

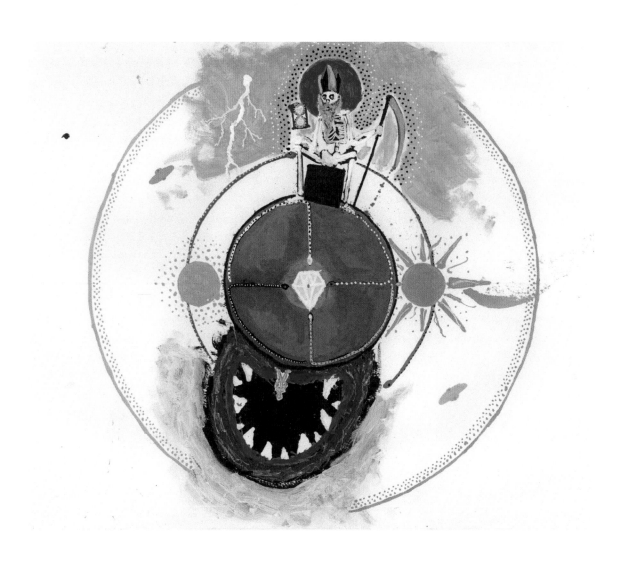

Rosen

The predominant image at the top of this twentieth mandala is of an evil, skeletal male figure whose head is full of rage. This figure is or was hurtful, and is connected with death, as is evidenced by the sickle and the hourglass made of serpents. There is also lightening in the upper left, which is the father quadrant. Counterbalancing the top is the bottom image of a huge, sharklike mouth with sharp teeth that bite and hurt the individual who is upside down. However, in the center of the image, the moon and the sun are once again balancing each other. The green and red serpent mandala connects the two traumas, the top and bottom images, as well as the feminine moon and masculine sun. UFOs seem to also be present, perhaps recalling the alien in earlier images, once again balanced in father and mother quadrants. Inside the central purple mandala, signifying royalty, is a smaller mandala made of four serpents which all connect and point toward the central diamond figure. In Buddhist imagry, the diamond represents ultimate spiritual enlightenment.

Jensen

Again with this image we return to feeling negative or oppressive side. The figure at the top is a tyrant king or pope, and a representation of the negative aspects of Saturn. He symbolizes time, limits, and constriction. He is a skeleton holding a scythe and an hourglass. He is a memento mori, a reminder that we all will die one day. He sits on a cube throne of lead. Just off to the left of the figure is a flash of lightning, the possibility for enlightenment in the storm. This figure could also be a representation of the negative father, Saturn was known to eat his children. At the bottom of the mandala, there is a large consuming maw (as in mandala #18), though this time the human figure stands outside of it and has his hands on his hips in a stance of defiance. The middle of the mandala holds a return of the diamond (mandala #17), and in its center there is a golden seed. Despite difficulty and pain, there at the center is the diamond heart and the potential for growth and resilience.

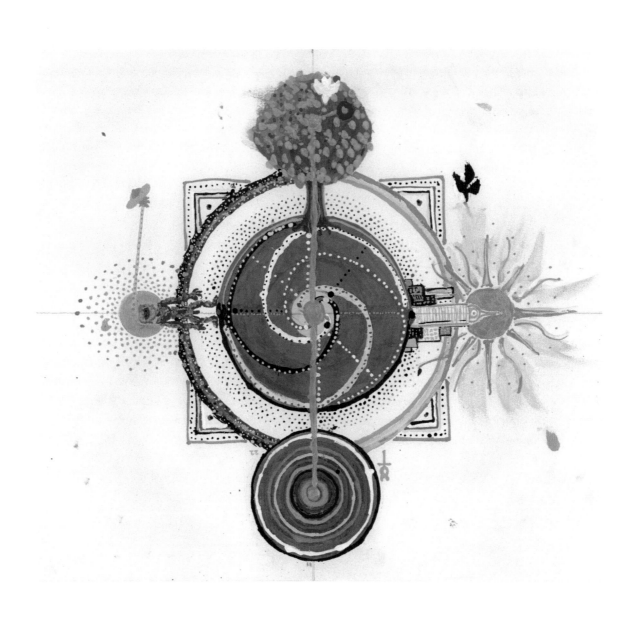

Rosen

In this, the twenty-first painting, the central spiral mandala with a purple background is indicative of his new identity. This identity connects to the tree, which is the self, and the rainbow circle which represents an underground ego. In the tree there is a dove and an apple. West and east of the central mandala are an ancient tree person with a phallus in a lunar, feminine space, counterballanced with a skyscraper, which is also clearly phallic, in the solar, masculine space. There seem to be extensions from both the lunar and solar bodies, with a UFO protruding from the moon, and a black raven emerging from the sun. Around the outer mandala is a square, or masculine, mandala. The square does not contain the circle, nor does the circle contain the square. Both are equally represented and fully integrated. Next to the rainbow circle is an upsidedown mercury symbol. Mercury is the god of commerce and communication, both of which fit with this individual's personal and professional goals.

Jensen

I feel like this image balances the previous image. There is a similar repeat in the purple central mandala, and a progression of the swirling of the serpents towards the middle. The moon and the sun are in the same positions to the left and right of the image, and it can be viewed rotationally from any perspective. This time the center holds more gold (maybe the seed has grown), and it is flowing up to the tree and fruit, and down towards a ringed mandala at the bottom which holds the seven colors of the rainbow, plus black and white, and silver and gold; eleven rings in total. The green man that was seen in burial in mandala #16, now alive and receiving alien gnosis through its pink laser beam. This could be another image of the self, like the other figures throughout the series, it seems to have more character than the figures in mandalas #8 and #13. The figure self-sacrificed, was buried, came back as embryo, then reborn as natural green entity. There seems to be a balance between the man-made (in the form of the city), and the natural (in the form of the green man). Often these two aspects are divided from one another but are dual sides of an underlying unity. Increasingly, after completing these mandalas, I would feel more centered and more integrated.

Rosen

This image, number twenty-two, again has the double mandala, with the masculine square connecting to, but not containing the circular, feminine mandalas. This is emphasized in the central mandala where you have the bodies of a woman and man integrated togther. She, the female figure, is holding the Eye of Horus, which is masculine, and he, the male figure, is holding a large pink flower, which is feminine. Additionally, outside the mandalas, an upright black dragon balances an upsidedown red serpent, and both have diamonds by their tails. There is more checkerboard integration at the bottom of the image, as he tries to figure out the game of life, and a seven layered beehive at the top as he proceeds with his graduate degree.

Jensen

This image is a continuation of integration, this time between the male and female sides. The green man has become fiery, and is holding a flower, a ten-petaled rose. The female side has blue skin, which reminds me of the goddess Kali; she is holding an eye of consciousness. In mandala #19, the two figures were merely holding hands, in this mandala the two sides of the figure have become one.

This is reminiscent to me of the beginning of the series, the only other time there has been a rose was the first mandala. There have been other flowers, lotuses, which have similar meaning. However, it seems significant that there have been no other roses. At the same time the first mandala also introduced the Star of David symbolism, which has occurred many times throughout the series, but here in the figure of the male and female conjoined is another way to represent the star in the active principle joining the receptive principle. Spirit integrated with soul. The beehive from mandala #19 has also reappeared, but this time it is at the top of the image (as opposed to the bottom previously), and it is pouring golden honey out onto the mandala. The four cosmic mountains have also reappeared, possibly pointing out the four directions. The four alchemical colors have also reemerged in the serpents winding throughout the circles of the image, and the checkerboard pattern coming into the foreground. I could imagine seeing the central figure dancing on the checkerboard. Though, the dragon and serpent to either side appear to be dangerous, I feel like they would be tamed by the inner figure. They also take the place of the columns or pine trees that have so often appeared throughout the series.

Rosen

Menorah number tewnty-three began as a dandelion, and then turned into an eye. The four menorahs are dandelion seeds being dispresed by the wind. They are balanced inside a ninesided star, which could be divided into three different Stars of David: black and white, black and red, red and white. The Eye of Horus appears in the center atop a tree. Traditionally, The Eye of Horus represents good health, protection, and power. This speaks well for this analysand.

In addition to those strong and auspicious features, The Eye represents the new ego or identity of this person, which integrates feminine and masculine in the black and white inside the eye. It looks as though everything is radiating from this new self, in yellow and pink dots. The four pink dots on either side again indicate integration of negative trauma that happened in childhood (around the age four). The repitition of the number four is significantly significant.

Jensen

The central image here began as a dandelion and transformed into an eye as I was continuing its creation. There are four dandelion seeds being blown out to the four directions. There is a nine-pointed star, and nine cosmic mountains with points of gold in their center. Nine could be a number representing completion as it is the final single digit number. White, black, and red are prominent again. This mandala came about after I found out about the need to move out of the state, and I would have to end analysis with David. At the time I felt grief for the unplanned end of our therapeutic relationship, and at the prospects of moving suddenly. Though, as opposed to feeling anxiety or fear about the change, I felt excited for leaning into the mystery of what will happen next.

Rosen

This final, twenty-fourth mandala is very significant and integrative. The diamond reappears in the center. The radiating burst of light from the diamond predicts his graduation, which successfully occurred, and his future as a loving father and caring therapist. Just behind the diamond and inside the final red serpant ouroboros, is the earth, which represents wholeness and grounding in the mother. This image represents hope rather than despair. Inside the yellow dotted mandala are abstract snow capped peaks which he has now successfully climbed. The counterbalancing rainbow quadrilaterals, pentagons, and hexagons again underscore the important events that happened at a young age.

In the final four quadrants, the upper left, paternal quadrant, is filled with a new galaxy, so he is owning his positive fathering of himself and his sons, as well as future patients. Balancing that, in the feminine, maternal quadrant on the lower right, is the purple hand of a woman holding the mercury figure, above which looms the Eye of Horus, or his new identity. In the bottom left corner, the unconscious, is the Star of David above the infininity symbol. Both are symbols of the integration of his personal and cosmic selves. In the upper right, the future quadrant, the reoccurring figures of the trees return, as well as the motif of the maze (now itself shaped like a tree). The trees balance one another, and at the center of the maze looms a dark figure, which is now centered, contained, and content. Finally, a number hovers to the left of the maze: simultaneously six and nine, it encompasses both the years of early trauma and the new freedom from it, pointing toward the balance of opposites.

Jensen

The final image in the series brings the words to mind, "it's turtles all the way down." This saying essentially means that there is always something underlying deeper exploration. Here there is a large colorful turtle shell holding up the earth. In the center of the earth, the diamond with the golden seed reappears, this time in an outward explosion of energy. This to me is similar to the previous mandala, releasing of the seeds to the wind. Though the expression in this mandala is more radiant and powerful. It feels both in the mandala and personally like a level of completion and mastery has occurred. A labyrinth reoccurs (there was another labyrinth in mandala #4), with two trees at the gates, and it seems as if it is pointing to further journeying. Also, it reminds me of a brain, maybe further intellectual development? I appreciated that the eye and the Mercury symbol returned, the Mercury symbol looks like a pen or a paintbrush in the purple hand of the cosmos. The galaxy was a new symbol to come into the series, and I was surprised at its appearance. It seems like its resonating with the world symbolism, a feeling of wholeness. Finally, the Star of David returned as a perpetually significant symbol in the series, and the main symbol the series began with. The end links to the beginning.

AFTERWORD

Jeremy Jensen brought these images to one of our final analytic sessions. They are significant because they embody his therapeutic experience and progress.

Rosen

He called the image above, "Dark Star," which is significant in that his new identity (in gold) is emerging from the tragic death of his father and righteous anger (in red). The golden spiral, his new identity, radiates.

Jensen

The final three mandalas are once again smaller. I think they encompass the whole of the series, in miniature. The first image, "Dark Star" represents the black phase of dissolution, or a black hole of negative feeling. This, in alchemy, is the nigredo and often represents the first phase in the alchemical process. This is the phase when I first began experiencing past trauma.

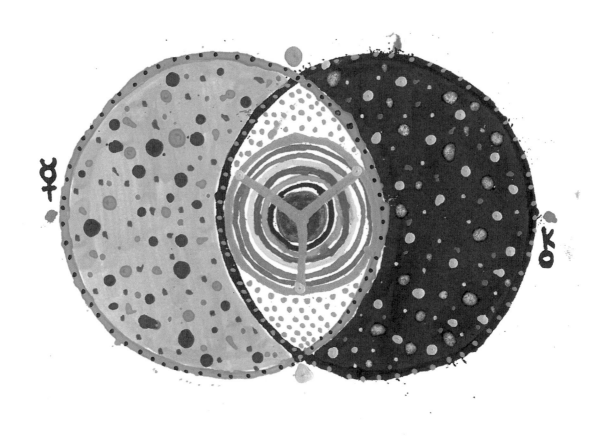

Rosen

The mercury symbol on the left indicates healing change, which is balanced by chronos (or an old soul) on the right. Both hold his new identity depicted by the eight rainbow circles in the middle mandorla. His central eye of identity is balanced by a sun above and a moon below. This figure represents enantiodromia, or the integration of the opposites, which is also captured by the image's title, "What Matters."

Jensen

The second image is titled: "What Matters." It depicts gold and the seven colors being born out of the mandorla, between the green of the Earth, and the starry black of the cosmos. It is the beginning of manifestation through the miracle of birth. This could represent the beginning of the integration of trauma, and the transformation into something new. The process of rebirth and renewal.

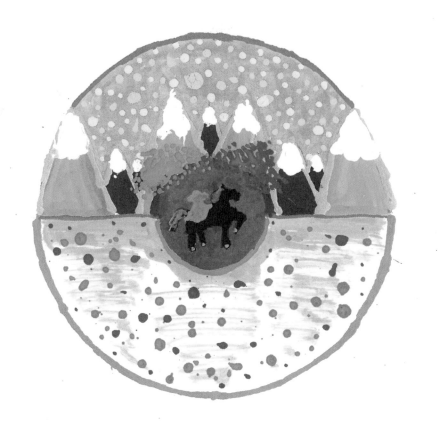

Rosen

This integrative mandala contains the analysand making progress on a black horse. The green fields of growth underlie everything, including the nine mountain peaks in the background. The orange in the top part of the mandala is filled with golden soul circles. He titled this image, "Demeter," or the mother god, since he is being reborn as his true self.

Jensen

Finally, "Demeter" depicts a rider on a horse between two trees, the rider representing the upper or divine self and the horse the animal or instinctive self. They are over the field of green, while nine mountain peaks are in the background. The image integrates the upper and lower, while exhibiting a sense of co-operation and mastery between dichotomous parts. This feels like an image of completion and triumph.

EPILOGUE

He who wants a rose must respect the thorn.

—PERSIAN PROVERB

On reflection, and in reviewing all the mandalas, it is evident that this analysand is involved in the ongoing work of individuation . . . a process toward wholeness. His analytic process bodes well for him, and he will surely be a supurb analyst.

Made in the USA
San Bernardino, CA
22 June 2020